THE DINER'S
COMPANION

Jeremy Wilson

ISBN: 1546619402
ISBN 13: 9781546619406
Library of Congress Control Number: 2017907861
CreateSpace Independent Publishing Platform
North Charleston, South Carolina

(I HOPE I'M NOT BEING TOO) FOREWARD

So you've decided to go out to eat. Fantastic. More importantly, you've decided to pick up this book (or some kind, wonderful person has taken it upon him- or herself to give you this book because *you need it*). Whatever the reason, kick up your feet and relax. This is a book about hospitality, after all, and in this field are a large portion of some of the greatest people you could ever meet—and we all want you to be happy. Neat, huh?

Now, that being said, we want you to be able to enjoy yourself to the fullest extent, and there are some things you should be aware of to help your experience at any restaurant become even more enjoyable. I was a bit apprehensive at first about even writing this book because it is a bit of baring of the hearts of the people who provide you with your experience. The subject matter we will go over has always been a tender issue about which not many know how to communicate properly, effectively, and objectively without losing their jobs *or* your business.

The answer is this catch-all book. Hopefully, most or all of this will seem like common sense to you, but these are issues that resonate throughout our industry. You'll be getting a very intimate view into a world you may have no idea even exists, hopefully with a good laugh or two along the way. With this book as a guide, you will be able to understand the driving thoughts and reasoning that predominate the restaurant culture. What is considered appropriate behavior, what should be avoided, and how to navigate the intricacies of any place you walk into are at your fingertips without you having to feel silly for asking and without us having to feel apprehensive about telling you.

The more this book hurts your feelings, the more you can learn from it and the better time you'll be having after taking these lessons to heart. Keep in mind that nobody is perfect; I will freely admit not only that sometimes there are mistakes made on our side, but also that we are sometimes guilty of things I will warn against doing when we go out. The important thing to remember is no one wants you to walk away with a negative experience. Compassion is an integral part of what we do, and unfortunately in this day and age, that is something that can't be purchased.

Please keep in mind that this book was written by someone who has spent the entirety of his career in US restaurants, and it is written for anyone who lives in or intends to eat in the United States. Please also keep in mind that while this is the most comprehensive compilation in existence, as a member of the service industry myself, I am always terrified I may have forgotten something.

Finally, remember that while this book is intended to be relatively lighthearted and informative, it is written by someone with a fairly dark and twisted sense of humor. Please take everything with a grain of salt, but in advance, I apologize.

CHOOSE YOUR ADVENTURE!
(or just keep reading the whole thing)

Feel free to use the rest of this space to write down page numbers you feel you need the most for quick reference, or even draw a picture of a cat or a flower, no judgement.

Section 1

BEFORE YOU EVEN WALK OUT THE DOOR

This prequel to your dining experience is one of the most important parts of your meal, one that is often sadly overlooked. This is the planning stage you should consider every time you want to eat out, where you have to ask yourself a lot of questions about your own expectations. There are very few places left in this country where a variety of cuisine and service styles are unavailable. Planning is a fickle thing; it can take you moments to months, depending on your particular circumstances, but it's true what they say: an ounce of prevention is worth a pound of cure.

The two main questions you should be asking yourself at this stage is what kind of food you want and whether you have the money to pay for it. If the answers are a fast-food burger meal and you've got five dollars on you, it's a pretty safe bet that you're all set to progress to the next step. For the rest of us, there are some other factors that need to be considered.

Let's first inspect your financial situation, since it's the easier of the two to deal with. I'm not going to look over your stocks and your budget projections for the month, so let me clarify. How much money are you willing to spend on this meal? This is important because it's going to determine the type of eating establishment you go to. We will go over each of these levels in greater detail later, but for now, let's focus on these summations. Now, this will vary depending on the cost of living in your area and how much you intend to eat, but generally safe ranges would be as follows:

One to eight dollars per person—You're headed for a QSR, or quick-service restaurant. Think drive-through, mall food courts, or food trucks; if it has a menu above a person looking at you from behind a cash register and counter, you're probably in the right place. These places will only be mentioned briefly as needed because they are fairly simple and straightforward. You get your food, you leave where you got your food from, and you eat your food. The majority of this book will focus on actual dining out, which can be a much more intricate experience.

Eight to twenty dollars per person—This range is your widest variety of locations and types of service you can get, as the majority of restaurants will fall into this range. From doing happy hour at a semiformal restaurant to a taqueria to a diner, twenty dollars will get you any kind of cuisine you can think of with someone else doing the work of retrieving your food from their kitchen and bringing it all the way to where you are seated (and sometimes even refilling your drinks for you too).

That's right; at this level of service, you will usually have someone waiting on you, and that means at this level the amount per person is also going to include a tip for the service you receive. Repeat: at this level, you need to factor not only the price of what you are eating but additional, unlisted costs into your equation. There will be much more on this later, but let's continue for now.

Twenty to fifty dollars per person—Now you're getting fancy! The type of locations you'll be attending in this range will almost completely be full service, some open only for dinner, and you may need to make a reservation ahead of time. If you're throwing down this much cash on a single meal, you'll probably want to research where you're going first anyway.

Fifty dollars plus per person—Hey, big spender! This is the slimmest level of availability as far as choices go, but what choices! For this amount of cash, you're going to almost assuredly be making a reservation, perhaps even months in advance. There might be a dress code at these establishments, and you can look forward to some massive steaks or a *prix fixe* (coursed) meal prepared by someone you may have even seen on the food network once or twice.

So now you've determined how much you're ready to spend. Fantastic. Now the real fun begins. Using the high-tech information network known as "the Internet," you can now easily find any style of restaurant within your price range that serves the type of food you'd like. If you or any dining companion is hard set on a specific type, American or Armenian, soul food or Seoul food, a quick search on just about any search engine will get you where you need to go. That is, of course, only if you can eat anything.

1 A

DIETARY RESTRICTIONS AND YOU: THE FIRST STEP

This is a sensitive subject for a lot of people, but knowledge is power, and the point of this booklet is to provide knowledge.

Let's start with the big one: allergies. Cow's milk, eggs, tree nuts, peanuts, fish, shellfish, soy, and wheat. Seven of these are understood by and large and are easy to avoid if you are aware that if you ingest them, they could kill you. However, in recent years, wheat has become more vilified than it probably deserves because of one reason: gluten.

Now, I have no intention of going ad nauseum into the subject, but there are three distinct fields in which the gluten/wheat epidemic can be broken down into. The first in order of severity is actual wheat allergy. This is the most severe but also the most isolated type, in which eating wheat can result in hives or anaphylactic shock. This is scary, but it's much more possible with people who are allergic to peanuts, tree nuts, fish, and shellfish. This allergy is usually prevalent in small children and can disappear by the time the child is about three years old. If you have this, you have an epipen. The good news is that most people who are allergic to wheat (about 80 percent) can consume other grains such as barley and rye, but again because of the severity, if you can't have something, you know what that something is.

The second type is celiac disease, where the body actually attacks the small intestine if the gluten compound is ingested. This is a genetic disease that affects roughly 1 percent of the human population, and like a wheat allergy, early detection is a relatively simple ordeal. Unfortunately, because of the trace amounts of gluten in almost everything, especially in a restaurant that uses flour and even in supposed gluten-free foods, people with celiac need to pay attention more closely than others when deciding where to eat. If they have one thing made with flour or coated with flour, it's almost certainly on everything, and seriously, they should avoid eating there. However, this disease is so uncommon that most people have no need to seek out gluten-free food, so why have we seen such a meteoric rise in the market for gluten-free items?

The answer is the third type, nonceliac gluten sensitivity. While the first two are serious conditions and easily identifiable, most people have only recently "discovered" they were gluten sensitive. Though this specific type is thought to affect roughly 6 percent of the population, it is also the one taken least seriously by members of the hospitality field and considered a "rich-person disease" that manifests in people with too much time and money who feel the need to be special beyond just buying all their food at whole foods.

You may wonder why this opinion exists so predominantly in the restaurant industry, but the answer is broken down into three simple parts. One, as mentioned earlier, the first two can cause bodily harm, not just temporary discomfort. Becoming gassy is not the same as your throat closing up. Two, these people who claim to have this condition are by and large the least educated on what they can and can't eat and will ask their server to figure it out for them. Three, because food knowledge is our job, most people in our field have researched the condition and found that the symptoms displayed by gluten-sensitive people are remarkably similar to those displayed by people who suffer a vitamin C deficiency, also known as scurvy. Studies have found adding vitamin c to sample cultures resulted in a notable drop in inflammation. I'm not a scientist, so you don't have to take my word for it, but please Google it, and drink more orange juice. Additionally, the scientist who "discovered" gluten sensitivity has even rescinded his claim after conducting a second study.

Now that that's out of the way, there are other less known allergies to food—cilantro, capsaicin, and others. But these should all be well documented for you from an allergy test you probably received when you were younger, and again, EpiPens mean serious business. Fortunately, with this knowledge you can plan your meal accordingly. If you have a shellfish allergy, you may want to avoid going to seafood places, and so forth.

If you find yourself in a situation where you have one of the major allergies, those will be readily listed on the menu, which nowadays can usually be found online, and will help you decide what you can and cannot eat. If the menu is not available or you have a less commonly known allergen, inform your server before ordering and he or she can help you make a selection and/or inform the kitchen appropriately. That's it. Simple and easy.

If you don't have a legitimate food allergy, what you have is called an "aversion" to a specific food. Contrary to the prevailing thought, you do not have to (loudly) declare yourself "specific food"-free. Just politely ask your server if the dish you want has the specific food in it and if it could be made without it. Don't expect a complete rundown of the menu in regard to your one specific food, though if your server has experienced this sort of question before or it's common enough in the restaurant, he or she may offer you a selection of dishes from the menu that can be made without the item in question.

1 B

RESERVATIONS?

This next step is also something most people will overlook but that needs to be factored in as the price point increases. Suffice to say, if you're going to a quick-serve place with a drive-through or a drive-in, you should be all right. Even if it's full, just wait **patiently** in line or go somewhere else.

The next level up can be a bit tricky, but usually only if you have a group of six or more. If you're planning a small company outing or an intimate birthday celebration, it is customary and polite to call **at least** an hour or two ahead to a place that lists itself as "no reservations required" to inform them how many people, and when you expect to arrive. This way they can preplan a table or section for you and your guests before you arrive, so there will be minimal or no wait time. In this type of situation, no matter what level you are at, it is recommended to have the party arrive as close together in time as possible, and it is proper etiquette to inform the establishment on any changes to the party size. This should be done at least by the time you arrive at the restaurant before anyone in your party is seated.

The third level is also tricky. When reservations are not required but recommended, you should consider not only your group size but also the time and day you plan on eating there. A party of four on a Tuesday may be able to walk in without a hitch at the same restaurant in which a party of two could face an hour's wait on a Friday night. In these situations it's always best to err on the side of caution and make a reservation, even on a Tuesday, as this will lock in your table, especially if there is a preferred area in which you would like to sit, such as a booth, near a window, closer or farther from a stage, and so forth. These places tend to get busier peak hours, and so a larger group should be booked earlier out, at least a week in advance to ensure proper seating time and location fits with your desires.

A special note for these locations—if there is a big event coming up, such as a popular musician's performance or a holiday like Mother's Day, you may want to consider placing the reservation even earlier on, perhaps as much as a month beforehand. It's also important you get the person's name whom you made the reservation with and remember the day and time you made it, if you don't have any other means of confirming the reservation was made. This way you know who exactly took your information in case somehow your reservation gets lost. It's unfortunate, but it does happen from time to time.

When you hit the tier of reservations only, it becomes much simpler, as your reservation is required, no matter the day or time. However, you may find yourself needing to book earlier on depending on the popularity of the restaurant. Some places may require only a day, others a week, and some even as much as a year in advance. It is for this reason that doing your research is so vitally imperative, as nothing is more disappointing than going to a place you were so excited to try on vacation turns out to be booked during the entire length of your stay. At some of these locations, a large group reservation may not be possible without a buyout, so call ahead. In these situations it's usually easier than reserving online, though online booking can be helpful to see how many open spaces are available and how far into the future the place is booked.

Of course, there are usually exceptions in almost any situation; a reservation-only place may have a bar area available for walk-ins. If you just happen to be out exploring, and again as long as you are willing to wait **patiently** for a spot, most restaurants won't turn you away. And of course, you can always go someplace else if you're really that hungry.

1c

BOOKING YOUR LARGE PARTY: A TABLE, A SECTION, OR A BUYOUT?

Have a group larger than six? Planning a company party, family reunion, reception, or any other large event takes a bit more planning. Ideally, large groups are best booked a month or more in advance. There are very few places that can handle a group of forty or more just walking in off the street unannounced. At the very latest, try to let the place you intend on visiting know at least a week ahead of time to prepare for your arrival. If they can accommodate you on that short notice, they will. If they can't or had another group that booked ahead, at least you will know and can try somewhere else instead of showing up to a disappointment

Trying to coordinate your group on its own takes a lot of effort to sync all the moving parts. The same is true for the restaurant staff. They need to schedule extra staff members, order extra or specialty food, and do everything else in their power to make sure your event goes exactly as you plan with them. Many places that can hold large groups will also have a catering menu available, removing the need for everyone to worry about what he or she wants to eat and providing your group with its more popular items at a reduced cost of what it would take to prepare the same amount of food one order at a time. A good restaurant coordinator will ask you lots of questions, leaving nothing to chance. Remember, the more you set ahead of time, the more you'll be able to enjoy yourself when your group gets there.

Odds are if you try to get any large group of people together in less than a week's time, you're going to have a lot of no-shows, which can be frustrating for everyone especially if the place you're going to reserves by a guaranteed minimum dollar amount you need to hit. If you plan a party of twenty and only four show up, those extra tables that sit empty are not only a loss of money for both the establishment, the server, and maybe even yourself, but it is also inconsiderate to other diners.

Imagine walking into your local bar and grill only to be told you would have to wait because there are no tables available, even though you can see three or four pushed together with no one at them. Would you want to return? Consideration for others is paramount when booking large groups; give your restaurant a heads up when your guest count goes down. Touching base a week before and the day before your event to finalize any details is a simple thing that can save everyone a headache.

Here is the breakdown for helping you decide which level you will be requiring for your group. First and foremost, please keep in mind that every restaurant is different and has different policies, unless it is a corporate chain that does not franchise its locations. Due to this fact, it is vital you call ahead and speak with a manager. But the factors that are required to consider are fairly consistent:

1. How large is your group? 2. How large is the restaurant? 3. What day/time are you planning your event? 4. How long do you plan to have your event in the building?

For these questions I will break it down into as much of a generalization as I can.

For groups of six to twelve, usually two to four tables can be pushed together without much of an issue **if the restaurant is large enough and prepared for your visit**. If the restaurant can seat sixty or more comfortably, you should be fine. If you're all just eating before going to a game or some other venue, time constraints shouldn't be an issue. Otherwise on a busy night (Thursday–Sunday, traditionally), it would be best if you planned on taking up to an hour and a half. On an off night (Monday–Wednesday), plan for two to three hours, depending on remaining seat availability. These time constraints are more a consideration to other people who may be very hungry and standing there at the front, watching you take up those tables and chat while your mostly finished desserts sit untouched.

If you figure your group will exceed this time limit, you may want to consider having a house party, as a catering company or a restaurant that delivers could provide you with the same amount of food and/or service without the rush. Be forewarned, though, that hosting a house party is often the gateway to attempting a career in the service industry. If you didn't plan on staying longer but you notice that you have, it's polite practice to compensate your server. More on that later.

For a group of thirteen to twenty, again depending on size and assuming a sixty-plus patron capacity establishment, they may have a section they prefer to seat large groups in that allows for you to have more elbow room between you and your companions and easier delivery of food and drink. Sections can be available for longer times than tables pushed together, provide greater privacy, and can be more comfortable for your group. The offset to this is usually an additional fee for the area and/or a limited menu to ensure not only an easier burden on the kitchen that prepares your food to be ready at the same time but also that you and your guests don't have to take the time poring over a menu and can focus on enjoying each other's company.

Sometimes, a section may not be available, but instead they may offer to seat you at multiple separate tables. If this is unsuitable to your party's needs, then this book has already earned its sticker price, because now you know you can find this out over a phone call or e-mail so you can make other arrangements (instead of becoming blustery in front of your group because the place you booked can't accommodate your desires). Usually, the only difference to reserving a section on a busy day or an off-day would be the additional cost of doing so. Though again this is something decided by the restaurant, they may even turn you down if they feel they cannot accommodate you and your group in the space you require.

Please note this is not because the restaurant doesn't want your business; it is in fact the exact opposite. They value your business so highly that they don't wish to offer more than they can reasonably accommodate and have no desire to allow you to receive substandard service just to make a few extra dollars that day or night. Most places operate on the idea that repeat business is more likely with great service than going over our expected sales one day with lousy service. It is, essentially, a matter of how much pride we have for the work we do.

If you cannot find a business in your area that can provide what you are looking for in the space provided for your cost point, you can consider VFWs, lodges, or any other small event space. Again, catering companies or a restaurant that delivers can be cost-effective depending on the level of service and food quality you desire.

For groups of twenty-one or more—or those more than a third of a restaurant's capacity—a buyout or section reservation are probably your only options, and again there will be places that may not offer such arrangements, which is why the preplanning stage is so vital. The company Christmas party is probably the best example of this, and the entire building could be at you and your guests' service for the higher price. Some establishments may only offer buyouts on days or hours they are closed to the public; others may only accommodate you for a maximum of four hours no matter what day you desire your event to be on.

Either way, once you find a location that accommodates buyouts, some of the considerations you will be talking about include not only price, but types of food service (appetizers only, coursed buffet, buffet, coursed meals) and entertainment needs (projectors or DJs) that may be required to be provided. This option allows for the most privacy and flexibility for what you are looking for. Optional venues would usually be banquet halls or country clubs, but in this instance, depending on location, a restaurant buyout may actually be a more cost-effective option, if it's available. Regardless, the more knowledgeable you are to your needs and the earlier you start looking into venues, the happier you will be with your experience once the final payment is made.

On a final note—sometimes emergencies come up, sometimes some people try getting into a variety of places, and sometimes people have to bail. If you have a group of six or more reserved at a place and you have to cancel, please call at least the day of or before your reservation. Keep in mind that if you have a larger party and a BEO or buyout was arranged, there may be a deposit you won't get back because that space was being held for you specifically to the detriment of other large parties. Think of them as contracts that you incur a fine for breaking. If your party is four or fewer, a call would still be nice, but it's not going to be the end of the world if you can't.

1D

A LOOK AHEAD

Now that you're properly prepared for your evening out, let's wrap things up with the planning phase. As mentioned throughout the section, the day you go out can influence the amount of business your destination is experiencing, which can negatively or positively affect the dining experience you are looking for. There are many other things you can take into consideration: ambient noise level from other diners, the amount of attention you're expecting, the type of atmosphere you want to dine in, and so forth. Those are dependent on your personal preference, but knowing to look into these things beforehand can turn any potential negative into a positive because you're prepared for what to expect when you get there.

Not only are there traditionally busier days of Thursday through Sunday, but there are prime eating hours of 11:00 a.m. to 2:00 p.m. for lunch and 5:30 p.m. to 8:00 p.m. for dinner every day. There may be more staff during these periods, but there may also be more customers. To make matters even more complicated, some places are busier when other places are slower. Your local watering hole may have its busiest day on Tuesday, when its tacos reign supreme, while that Chinese place you've been meaning to try might be a ghost town that night—but it's always too packed on the weekends. Use this knowledge to avoid the crowds if you so desire, but we will touch on hours in the next chapter in greater detail.

One special note: as you're preparing for your night out, if it's an occasion where you're getting dressed up and going out after dinner, or just for dinner, stop before you apply your perfume or cologne. Just stop.

While we understand the desire to smell nice, and getting cleaned up before going out into public is always a good idea, there are two huge reasons to avoid spraying yourself down with your favorite scent. First and foremost, a bit of science for you: most of what you taste is actually determined by your sense of smell. Following this logic, if all you can smell is your fragrance, you're cheating yourself of the wonderful flavors of your cuisine. Secondly, if you're overloaded with fragrance, you're not the only one who will be able to smell it; other guests around you will also be unable to fully enjoy their meals if all they can smell is what you're wearing. As a consideration to all the other diners in your area, if you do want to smell that strongly, please wait to apply until after you've eaten.

If you absolutely must apply fragrance, spray a quick press on to one wrist, rub your other wrist against it, then run your wrists behind your ears. That's all you need; it will last longer, and only the people who get in close to you will be able to smell it, which is what you should want.

SECTION 2

KNOW WHAT YOU'RE GETTING INTO

Now is as good a place as any to share a tiny history lesson with you. I realize your stomach is probably starting to growl, so we'll make this as brief as possible. Journey with me back a few thousand years or so to where we widely source as the starting point of hospitality, ancient Greece.

The Greeks, being god-fearing people (and having many gods to fear), developed a system for welcoming strangers into their homes—partially because Zeus was a protector of strangers and travelers, and partially because any stranger could be a god in disguise. Welcoming a stranger in could result in received gifts, whereas shunning a stranger could result in the incursion of a god's wrath. For most Greeks, this was a fairly easy choice. The practice of hospitality was so important that it was the basis of their nobility and social standing, and it had two basic rules:

The respect from host to guest: The host must be hospitable to the guest and provide him/her with food and drink (and a bath, if required).

The respect from guest to host: The guest must be courteous to the host and not be a burden.

Both parties following these two simple rules ensures the guests are shown respect, have their needs met, and are treated as **equals**. The laws are so fundamentally sound that they are evident in the history of almost every surviving culture in varying degrees and are the basis of the hospitality industry today (minus that bit about a bath, somewhere along the lines it became rude to suggest someone could use a wash). Indeed, modern pubs originated with literal public houses, homes that opened up for the public to come and relax, and to this day there are still restaurants being run in the same building the owner's family calls home.

It is because of this underlying mentality that restaurants are singularly different from any other type of business. The people who work there are not at their office; they are in their homes. Their coworkers are their large, dysfunctional family, and they spend more time there and with those people than they do at their own homes with their own families. When you walk in through the doors, you're not going into a store; no matter what the building may look like, the soul of any restaurant is a home.

The point of this little history lesson is to establish a mind-set when walking into your chosen restaurant. Not only should you feel welcome and at ease, but you should also treat it and act as you are a guest in someone else's house. If you take nothing else away from this booklet, please take that to heart. Whether you think of it as your grandma's house, your best friend's house, or someone whose house you are visiting for the first time, you are a guest in someone's home.

It's important to make these distinctions because sometimes, in our effort to make everyone feel as welcome as possible, a sense of entitlement comes over a few people now and then. But when you think of being a guest, you don't yell at Grandma because you don't get your way. You don't slap your friend's sibling on his or her ass if you want to keep your friendship, and you don't vandalize a stranger's home unless you want to leave the place in handcuffs.

As such, it is important here to stress four essential things as a mnemonic device to ensure an enjoyable experience in an environment based on reciprocal altruism. **When going out to eat, remember these four "ates."** Please be *literate and articulate; communicate* your needs, and please be *considerate.*

As you read through the following three chapters, you will begin to notice how all three are closely interconnected, and though each is a start-to-finish progression throughout the meal, each section contains the individual reasoning and explanations for the three "ates" instead of meshing them all together. It is my intention that explaining things in this way will help you be able to make those connections yourself to more fully cement the ideas in your mind.

SECTION 3

BEING LITERATE IN A RESTAURANT

I f you have made it this far in this booklet, it's fairly safe to assume you are capable of reading. Congratulations. For the convenience of those few who are capable of this tremendous feat, most restaurants have a bevy of information readily available to you without you having to say a single word. From the outside in, let's go over what you can expect to find just about anywhere with your amazing ability to comprehend written words.

3A

OUTSIDE

Open or **Closed**: Usually, this may be either a sign flipped one way or another, or a neon or some other lit sign. If the sign is flipped to Open or the Open light is turned on, that means the restaurant is indeed open for business, the doors are unlocked, and you can go in and purchase food. If you see this sign indicating that they are indeed open and you can make it through the door, there is no need to ask if they are open or not. Even if they seem to be working on some sort of setup, even if there is no other person in the restaurant, Open means you are welcome to come in and eat.

Conversely, if the Open sign is turned off or the closed sign has been flipped, regardless of whether the lights are still on, there are still people inside eating, or food is still coming out to tables, they are no longer accepting new guests. For most places, no amount of haggling can be done to change this to accommodate you, and it's considered bad manners to make such an attempt. The reason this is considered rude is that though they are there to take care of you, they have lives outside of work just like you do.

Imagine if a client or customer came to you after you had finished for the day and asked you to work an extra two hours for five dollars. Now, I realize that some lucky folks are on salary and make the same amount no matter how much they work and thus are always available to work. Restaurant workers do not fall into this category. Many have second or even third jobs, college schoolwork, and/or a family to take care of.

Fortunately, there are alternatives. Most everywhere you go there is always someone serving food at any point of the day; there may even be a twenty-four-hour restaurant nearby, and some places may even be able to suggest nearby alternatives if you ask politely.

Please always keep in mind that any person who is out there, from a CEO to a ditch digger, is trying to make something of his or her life and contribute to society in whatever way he or she is capable. The person's time is as equally important to him or her as yours is to you.

As simple as the Open/Closed sign is, there is a major caveat that needs to be taken into consideration in addition to the sign: the hours of operation.

Hours of Operation: These are the normal business hours of the restaurant, and they are usually posted for your convenience to inform you of when you are welcome to come in and enjoy their service. Usually they appear at least on the front door and on-line, but it's not a regulated thing. These are again location specific and sometimes subject to change. For instance, though we are notorious for being open on many days out of the year when no one else is, some restaurants may close on certain days of the week, holidays, or for emergency repairs or restoration. Some places may also extend their hours of operation for special events, opening earlier for a big sports game or staying open later to celebrate New Year's Eve. Usually, these days will be marked approximately a week in advance for their regular customers.

Likewise, depending on the season, they may be opened longer or shorter hours based on the amount of business they expect throughout the week. There are even some places that will shut down early if the amount of business they received during the day does not merit remaining open.

Having a good idea of the hours of operation for your intended restaurant is helpful in the instances where the restaurant gets very busy before they close and don't have the time to turn off or flip their open sign immediately. If you see an open sign at 9:05 p.m. and the hours of operation are only till 9:00 p.m., this may be one of those instances in which you should be mindful of the posted hours. Though, if you want to take a chance, instead of asking if they are still open, you may ask if they are still taking new guests. Again, since every place is unique, some may even say yes, but prepare yourself emotionally for a no.

Dress code/smoking policy/firearm policy: These are usually pretty self-explanatory. You should be fully dressed, only smoke in designated areas (if it's a smoke-free establishment, usually at least ten to fifteen feet away from any door or window), and for most cities and some entire states, usually only on-duty, uniformed policemen are welcomed with a firearm holstered.

Requests for consideration: Not all restaurants are single units surrounded by parking lots or in high-density urban areas. Very many are nestled within neighborhoods of people who may not keep the same hours as the restaurant. These establishments will often ask that you please keep your voices down and generally not cause a ruckus in consideration to those neighbors when you are outside of their establishments or, if they have open windows, inside as well. Even though restaurants themselves are businesses, they are also members of their community and want to maintain a courteous and ongoing relationship with their neighbors. No one likes noise complaints. Not the business, not the residents, and certainly not the police. Please keep it down.

Display menu: Found especially in high foot-traffic areas, there will often be a menu posted outside near the entrance. These are there if you are just wandering through and wanted to check the restaurant out to see what kind of food and pricing they offer. If you see one of these and aren't familiar with the store, feel free to take your time to look it over. Be mindful of whether you are near the door and make sure that you are not blocking the door or doorway, as it may swing open quickly, and someone may collide with you. On that note, please be careful when approaching or opening a door, for your safety and the safety of others.

Outside seating: Generally, if there is a barricade around the patio, whether or not you can easily open a gate to it or not, it is implied that you need to first go inside the restaurant. Even if the patio is easily accessible, there may be signs instructing you to go inside first. There are a multitude of reasons for this.

First and foremost, many places may need to be aware that there is someone outside that requires service, as often many blind spots throughout the building can inhibit seeing you there and delay your dining experience. Even if there are already guests out on the patio, the host may be holding menus that you will want to have. It's always better to ask first unless you're already familiar with the policies of the restaurant you're entering.

Secondly, the restaurant may not be staffed properly to accommodate seating outside, and the patio may be closed for the season or the day. Though unlikely, it can happen. Most likely, however, the reason for checking in first is because there might be multiple servers on at one time, each with their own sections (imaginary lines that define their work areas) to ensure that each server has an equal opportunity to make a certain amount of money and that you as a guest have an equal opportunity for excellent service. This will be covered in greater detail in the next section.

Parking restrictions: In some areas, parking space is at a premium. But certain other areas, such as next to a fire hydrant, need to be kept clear for safety considerations. Some places may offer to valet your vehicle to save you the hassle of finding a parking spot; others may post signs where it is not clearly labeled by the city (so you don't get issued a ticket or towed), and some have private lots. You can ask any judge—"No parking" never includes "unless you promise you're just going to be real quick."

Private lots will usually state that parking in designated areas or the entire lot is for their customers only. This is done primarily so that people who are there to enjoy their dining experience don't have too far to travel between their car and the establishment—it is an extra consideration for their guests. Following that, most places will have your vehicle towed away if you are not there to eat at the restaurant because the space is reserved for their customers, whether the lot is full or not.

Imagine you're taking your grandparents to their favorite spot, but instead of being able to park ten feet from the door so they don't have to travel far, you're forced to park five blocks away because some other person was using the spot because the lot across the street was full. Whether you're only going to be two minutes or fifteen minutes at a nearby location, their lots could fill at any moment, and what you are doing is being inconsiderate to the guests of that establishment and the rules laid out by the proprietors of the area.

However, with that in mind, most places won't mind if, after eating and communicating with your server or some other employee of the establishment, you frequent nearby businesses for an additional half hour or so. The difference is this: not only have you already invested your money in the restaurant but you have also communicated your intent so that they know you will be occupying the space a little longer. If they are unable to accommodate you at that point, they will let you know so as to avoid anything unpleasant to sour your experience with them.

Push/pull (entering/exiting the establishment): Again, most would think this to be a fairly simple explanation, but you may be amazed how many people on a daily basis don't take the time to read one little word and ram themselves, often multiple times, into a door clearly labeled "pull" or tug fruitlessly on a door labeled "push" to the side. Likewise, there may be additional information as in "watch your step," meaning there is either a step up or down as you enter. Please be mindful that the reason these signs are in place is not to tell you how to live your life, but how to safely navigate the complexities of that particular doorway.

Everyone, the author included, has had at least one instance of this, for whatever reason (not enough coffee, too much booze, preoccupied with a phone call, or some other external factor), and the point of this is not to make you feel silly for not being able to operate a very simple thing. It's just a reminder that keeping your eyes peeled for visual instructions can only be a good thing.

3B

INSIDE

When you enter a restaurant for the first time, things may get a little tricky, as directions may not be written out for you. Fortunately for you, however, *The Diner's Companion* is here to save the day! Once you have safely cleared the threshold, **stop** and observe your surroundings. You may either need to seat yourself or wait to be seated.

Seating yourself: There are two easy ways to determine if you need to seat yourself. The first is that when you walk in, there is a sign that says "Please seat yourself." Secondly, if there are ushering lines or simply a counter that says "Order here." For the counter service, you need only to walk up, place your order, and then find a seat. If there is no clear indication, please wait for an employee to notice you and direct you as required. Slightly more complicated restaurants may have no clear indication, so you'll have to gauge it by the type of establishment you are entering. If it's a low-key pub or bar, you may be expected to seat yourself. Higher-end dining may just not have room for signage, and it may be better to wait.

However, if instructed by a sign to seat yourself, or if an employee instructs you to sit anywhere you like, as reasonable as the following explanation may seem, please keep this simple suggestion locked in your head: **don't sit at a dirty table.** Please reference this in section 5, as a more detailed explanation is provided.

If you have this booklet with you and you are referencing things on the fly, you may skip to the next section for now.

Waiting to be seated: If you have come inside to get a patio (outside) seat as instructed, you are already aware you need someone to seat you in an appropriate area, even if they lead you back out the way you came in, even if the area is anywhere you like. Kudos to you for following proper procedure; we appreciate it more than you can imagine! If you are not intending to sit outside or there is no outside seating to be had, you also have two very obvious signs to look for.

As mentioned earlier, if there is a sign that says "Please wait to be seated" or something of a similar nature (please sign in, please check in with host, etc.), you are most assuredly on top of what you need to do. However, if you see a podium, desk, or any other sort of furniture near your path, this is what we refer to as a host stand. Even if there is no host or hostess there at that particular moment, there will be one shortly, and we appreciate your patience. If you see an open book or sheet asking you to sign in, this is done to ensure if multiple parties arrive while the host is away, they are aware of the sequence of your arrival and will seat on a first-come, first-served basis. The rare exception to this is if you have arrived early for a reservation and others have arrived on time for theirs.

Again, if you see no sign, no furniture, and are unsure of what to do next, it is still recommended you wait until you are noticed and addressed to either seat yourself or that they will be with you in just a moment.

Checking out the menu/specials: If you are window-shopping for a potential place to eat and no menu is on display outside, there may likely be one inside, near the front door. In this instance, again please wait patiently to be acknowledged and request to see a menu, even if you can see where they are being stored. If one is not on display, it is customary to ask, to be polite. Once you have possession of a menu, if it is a takeaway menu, you may leave with it, but if it is covered, in a book, or is laminated, it is a house copy and meant to stay on premises, so please step out of the way of any aisle or doorway before you start browsing as a safety concern for yourself and others.

If you are already seated, there will either be menus already on the table or placed by the host on the table for you. If it is a counter service or limited menu, this information may be on a large board over the counter, on a table tent (those small, often double-sided advertisements next to the condiments or as a centerpiece), or on a wall somewhere, usually closest to the entrance. Most often, it will be some combination of these that each focus on a particular offering the restaurant would like to highlight. Specials are often listed above the counter or bar only, or the main menu may direct you to ask the server to verbally explain it to you, or it may even have its own information packet already on the table. Again, it can be tricky, but if you know where to look and how to read, all this wealth of information can be available to you without anyone needing to say a single word.

Restrooms, this way: Of all the sneaky and cunning information in a restaurant, this easily takes the cake. The best of us literate folk can still be caught off guard looking for these elusive signs. Usually they are hanging above eye level or at eye level on some nondescript wall; if it is an emergency when you are walking in, or you cannot identify its location while staying seated and swiveling your head around (more on the reason for that later), it is perfectly understandable if you need some direction by asking an employee (even if it becomes painfully obvious after receiving his or her instructions; nobody's perfect and we completely understand). Again, if you know the signs and the areas to look for them, you too can become a super restroom sleuth!

Important Note on Restrooms: Not all restrooms are created equal; in some areas you may feel free to come in and just use their restroom and leave, while other locations (usually in high-density urban areas) may require a key or some other way to unlock them because they are for customers only. This is not because they think you are a disreputable person, but because of policies put in place due to a high amount of vagrancy in the area. These vagrants can make a mess of the facilities, turning the most spotless restroom into a sty, threatening the safety of other restroom users, even using stalls for drug use, which could lead them to overdose. Please be considerate—if you really have to use the restroom, order something cheap and quick, like a cup of coffee; pay for it; and then use the facilities.

The bill: The most complicated of all reading material, the bill provides information on what you ordered, how much each item cost, and the total amount you are **obligated to pay** the establishment for the items you consumed during your visit, as well as any discounts or additional fees that may have been applied. It often contains additional information such as the business name and location, who your particular server was, and perhaps even a quaint little departure note like "Thank you!" or "Please come again!" It is tricky because it combines words and numbers and expects you to be able to understand how they correlate, and sometimes items can be incorrectly entered by accident, so it is vitally important to check that all the information is correct. Even more confusing, sometimes all the extras don't show up in print, and the total may not add up correctly. Fortunately, your server should be able to explain any discrepancies to you. More on the bill and you later.

3 c

THE REASONING BEHIND IT ALL

There are a multitude of reasons all this information is laid out clearly in front of you. I may not cover them all, but here are the main reasons we rely so heavily on written words in restaurants.

Safety: By far, this is the reason that stands out most. Most restaurants, at their peak hours (and the rare few that never have off-peak hours) are a bustle of activity. Guests are coming and going, and the staff is going through a very well-rehearsed dance to avoid running into each other while still attending to all their duties as quickly as possible. Things get dropped (wet floor), people can trip (watch your step), health reminders (wash your hands; it's not a good idea to eat rare chicken), and any other number of things could go wrong at any time. Indeed, the highest law in almost any restaurant is Murphy's Law, and the signs that we have are there to mitigate it as much as possible, so the staff can focus on more immediate needs for their voices.

Accessibility: Especially for first-time guests, we realize that all the information can be daunting to process all at once, and some people need references to go back to while making decisions. Because the information is all written down for you, you have the most standard information of not only what is available but what most items consist of, and you can be sure you know exactly what you are ordering and how much it will cost.

Time: The thing that is most vital in a restaurant's success is the thing that is the most sensitive to mention. The truth of the matter, though, is that the less time an employee needs to explain things to a table, the more time they have to get those things not only to that specific table but also to the other tables around them. There are countless instances throughout history, perhaps even in your own experience, where one group of customers didn't get their food or drinks in time because another table was taking up all the employees' time asking questions that they could have easily figured out for themselves, had they only taken the time to read. Hot items can only stay hot for so long, and cold items are exactly the same way, and both of them are ready when they're ready and lose their maximum enjoyment the longer they sit without being delivered to you.

Now, a server will never (and should never) tell you that you are wasting their time. Even if you notice yourself or someone else in your group holding up your server to ask things such as whether he or she knows specifically where the food was grown or things of that nature, if you apologize for it, the server will assure you it's not a problem at all. If it's relatively slow, he or she may have more time to talk, and there are probably even those who enjoy having that conversation. So don't take this as an indication that no one wants to talk to you; it's quite the opposite.

There are a lot of things the server will have to communicate with you, and in many cases, he or she may even engage you in small talk, but the more time the server takes with you informing you of what is right in front of you, which he or she is more than happy to do, the more likely the person becomes inattentive to his or her other guests. Many servers will master the ability to excuse themselves from a conversation by directing you to the menu to ensure that all of their guests receive equally attentive service.

SECTION 4

BEING ARTICULATE (AND KNOWING HOW TO COMMUNICATE) IN THE RESTAURANT

While not nearly as lengthy as the other sections, this is actually one of the easiest and most effective ways to ensure you get what you want—by knowing how to communicate your needs and thoughts clearly. As the old saying goes, clarity of speech reflects clarity of thought.

The staff members are there to help you receive the best possible experience you can have, but they are not mind readers. You may or may not be surprised how many negative reviews you see online have come from people who didn't mention a single thing being wrong during their visit. Depending on circumstance, please be mindful of this; from an initial phone conversation to when you're walking out the door, please be as clear and concise as you can.

For example, when placing your order, if there are three salmon choices (a grilled salmon, a salmon cake, and a salmon soufflé, or whatever), if you ask for "the salmon," the server may ask you to specify, or you may end up getting the grilled salmon when you wanted the salmon cake. Taking the time to specify exactly what you want is the best way to get exactly what you want. Of course, we already went over being literate, so if you see two or more menu items with similar names, you know which one you want.

Often, all it takes is one additional word to clarify your order. Believe it or not, some people who can't stop talking about everything else suddenly become minimalists when it comes time to actually ask for anything. Most servers will repeat your order back to you just to make sure you're both on the same page or ask you about sides or cooking preparations. If what they're saying doesn't sound like what you wanted, they may be thinking of some other dish. Getting your order nailed down before they leave the table at this point in time will save you the trouble of waiting for your meal to be remade while the rest of your table has their food.

Also, you may want to make sure you remember what you ordered. Sometimes food orders that are almost identical get taken to the wrong table; sometimes people forget and think they ordered something other than what they actually did. It's not a huge deal, but we want you to have the food you ordered (and whoever ordered what got brought to you to have what they ordered too), so if you think you received the wrong dish, point it out as soon as you notice so it can be corrected.

If you have children with you who are shy or who cannot speak clearly enough to be easily understood, you're not doing anyone any favors by forcing them to order for themselves. Putting them on the spot will not increase their confidence, nor will taking two minutes to order a kids' cheeseburger you could have ordered for them in ten seconds improve the mood of the hungry child or the server who is already backed up with his or her tables.

If there is a language barrier of any sort, you are absolutely more than welcome to point to the exact menu item you want to order. For example, if this is your first time eating in a Korean place and you see a dish you're excited to try but have no idea how to pronounce it, point at the item and give it a shot, if you want to try pronouncing it; even if the server corrects you, it's just to let you know how to say it in the future. The person will not think any less of you for not knowing how to speak Korean; I promise.

On the opposite end of the spectrum, if you went on vacation in Japan once or lived there for years, you see the English equivalent of something on a menu, and the server is speaking to you in perfect English or English tinged with Spanish or German or anything other than Japanese, don't order the dish using the proper Japanese name because the server may not know it like that. No one is going to be impressed that you had the dish and know the right way to say it. You're in an American equivalent and will get the American equivalent of the dish if you order with the name it has been given in English. If it comes up in natural conversation with your server, great, fantastic. If you feel insulted that someone doesn't know everything you know and feel the need to belittle them for it, you're not doing yourself any favors as a human being and are really just coming off as a smug jerk.

Tying in with the next section, articulating also extends to feedback on the meal and your overall dining experience and will come into play in chapter 7 of the book, "Food Blogging and You, or To Yelp or Not To Yelp, That Is the Question." Unless you are in a quick or counter service establishment, shortly after your food is delivered to you, your server and oftentimes a manager will approach to check in to see how your meal is going. This query is not to make sure you're only able to barely choke down the food (and despite popular conception, we don't plan this visit when you're mid-bite). Instead of saying, "It's fine" or "Good," **politely** make some waves by identifying anything that may be below your expectations.

It may be worth mentioning at this point that your expectations frame your experience. I'm fairly confident when I say the next Gordon Ramsey is not working at your local Denny's, and even if he or she were, if the person doesn't adhere to the consistency that the company expects, he or she might not be for long.

Realize that some places have saltier soups than others, and sometimes a dish is made to someone else's tastes than your own. Sometimes, a dish you've known your whole life may be made in a completely different way but still be given the same name. Don't panic; you don't have to settle for something you're not happy with. If you are specific enough on why you don't like the dish, being too salty or spicy or sweet, your server can either have the dish remade to your liking or offer an alternative dish that would be more suitable for your palate. Also realize that cooked medium should always be medium, and french fries should never come out cold; if you've had the dish before at that place and it tastes off, **stop eating** and let someone know immediately. More on this later.

If there is a problem with your server's personality or he or she rubs you the wrong way, ask to speak to a manager immediately, again being as specific as possible to any problem you feel is interfering with your enjoyment of not just the meal but your overall experience at the restaurant. No one can see everything going on all at once, and most managers will be glad you drew the problem to their attention so that they can fix it. If you notice the restrooms are out of soap or paper or are dirty, this is information they need to be aware of so they can correct it. Think of it as pressing a pause button when you see or taste something wrong and then letting the staff correct it and press play for you. Hopefully, this will only happen once if at all during your visit, but we would much rather be aware of a problem immediately than after we can't do anything about it.

Section 5

BEING CONSIDERATE IN THE RESTAURANT

As you may have noticed by now, I've been mentioning consideration fairly frequently already. That is because so much of what we do is based on the consideration of your needs, often to the detriment of our own. This section really is what the whole book is about. However, in this section we will go into greater detail, going through the entire dining experience from start to finish. Through that time, we ask that you please try to be as considerate to us as we are trying to be to you.

This section is no doubt where most of the controversy occurs between guests and restaurants. It is both the easiest and hardest for me to write because there are so many people out there who **need** to know these things, but at the same time, I worry if it's coming off as a lecture on how to live your life. With that said, keep in mind that this book is essentially a tool, and like any tool, it can be used properly or improperly (for good or evil), depending on the person wielding it. I'm in no way demanding you become a decent human being, nor am I implying you are not already. This is more a guideline to interacting with others in general, and to most, I am sure that most of these suggestions will seem like common sense. These "don't" points we are about to go over are on the same level as "don't cut in line," "don't pee in public pools," and "don't shake babies to get them to stop crying." You can still do them, but other people might not appreciate it.

Keeping that in mind, I am going to take you through from seating to leaving a restaurant with the understanding that we have already discussed making reservations if you have a large party and how to identify a host stand. The first section is actually a carry-over from the encounter mentioned previously when you are directed to seat yourself.

5A

DON'T SIT AT A DIRTY TABLE

While to most this would seem common sense, you have no idea how often someone who works in this sort of environment will see the opposite action occur. You may also not be aware of how it can be viewed as an insult that can affect your entire dining experience with your server. So let me explain: the food-service industry is regulated by the health department, and as a result, most establishments are **obsessive** about cleanliness. They operate under the assumption that, likewise, you would prefer eating at a clean table than a dirty one, and being able to provide you with a clean spot to eat is a matter of pride.

To be fair, there are some places you will go in to eat where every single table is already covered in crumbs. That is most likely because in those cases the counter service may indicate you are required to clean up after yourself in consideration of the people who come in after you, and none of the people who came in before you were feeling especially considerate. These places may not have price points in place to ensure someone is maintaining the tables, or it may be simply that the cleaning of tables happens much less frequently than the amount of times those tables get used. These situations cannot always be avoided unless taking your food to go and sometimes require that you take the extra effort to clean the table before as well as after you eat. No, it is not your responsibility to clean up after anyone else, but it is a sort of pay-it-forward consideration for your fellow diners to clean up after yourself. Even if no one else around you is doing it, you can take some small comfort in that you made a small gesture for someone else.

All that aside, in places that allow open seating or the ability to seat yourself and *do* have the staff to clean up after you (even if they are unable to do so immediately after you leave), please don't select a table that has another person's dirty dishes and other refuse on it. Allow a server or bus person to clean it off first; it is considered to be part of their job and a part of why you pay them extra in the form of a tip. Much more on this later. However, when you sit at a dirty table, there are usually a few possible thoughts that run through a server's head.

One, you are a slob, and you enjoy sitting in other people's garbage. This is an extremely distasteful idea for anyone who has spent so much time maintaining his or her own cleanliness as well as the cleanliness of his or her workplace. Two, you are too oblivious to realize that where you are sitting is dirty and should not be seated at. This is mostly dreaded because no one wants to think of someone who will be responsible for paying him or her for work is completed is so detached from reality (if you don't realize you shouldn't sit at a dirty table, you may not realize you also need to tip). Third, you are stubborn or feel so much self-entitlement that you will only sit in a certain table, regardless of whether it's clean or not.

The fourth and most unpleasant thought is that you are nonverbally communicating to the servers that they are not doing their jobs fast enough, that they willfully permitted you to sit in filth because they did not care about your dining experience. By this line of reasoning, it is also implied that you did not possess the patience to wait for a table to be cleared and have no respect for the service that person is trying to provide not only for you but also to all his or her other guests.

Since no one wants to presume you as a slob, especially if you look well dressed and clean, or that you are obtuse, the most common result is that the server processes your actions as some combination of the third and fourth explanations and is, rightly or not, offended by your actions. It may seem like a silly thing, but it can be a huge pet peeve that could be easily avoided once people actually are made aware of it. Because of the peculiarity of the hospitality industry, however, no one wants to be the one to tell you about it.

To avoid this negative interaction, now that you are aware of it, there is a relatively simple solution. Communicate to the employee your intent to sit at the specific table and wait patiently for the person to clear and reset it. He or she will be grateful that you took the time to address your request to him or her and will accommodate you as soon as possible. The person will not let any new arrival sit there before you do once he or she knows that is the table you desire, so you needn't worry about letting it slip through your fingers. Because you displayed knowledge about proper procedure and the respect to communicate your needs, the server may feel more inclined to go out of his or her way to accommodate future requests in your current and future visits.

As a special note, once you have indicated the area you wish to be cleaned so that you may sit and enjoy yourself, please do not hover by the area in question. Again, rest assured that the employee realizes that you want to be the next person to sit there and will not let anyone else sit there until you are done and gone. The person does, however, require a certain amount of space and time to clear the table as quickly as possible. Imagine that you are trying to sweep up an area covered in dirt, and now place someone directly in that area watching you. It becomes slightly unnerving and more time consuming.

5B

DON'T HELP YOURSELF TO
WHATEVER YOU WANT

This is also a fairly commonsense point of etiquette, with the exception of those wonderful, sweet, delicious buffets (which still have some things that may require a staff member to acquire or prepare for you on request) and counter-service spots (that may have "grab and go" sections similar to airport kiosks or convenience stores). But even those establishments may have their own levels of service, so if it's your first time at that specific restaurant, it's polite to ask first.

There are three big reasons for this, the first being common courtesy. Be aware that the restaurant is not yours, and even if it was, most owners don't actually wait on themselves. Again, it helps to think of restaurants as public houses. If a stranger came into your house and helped him- or herself to a beer out of your fridge, you would probably be upset, and no matter how great a person that stranger may turn out to be, that initial impression won't go away because it's just an incredibly rude thing to do.

There is a world of difference between taking something you want and asking for someone to give that same thing to you—especially if you're taking something that was being prepared for someone else. Imagine if you waited patiently for a burger to be prepared exactly how you like it, only to have someone grab it before it arrived at your table because he or she saw it and decided he or she wanted it. Or your pitcher of beer never arrived because someone took it from the service area before your server got to it. In effect, you now have to wait longer because someone else didn't feel like the rules applied to him or her.

Secondly, there are people being paid to do that job for you, like people who pump your gas, clean your house, or handle your gardening. Even if you yourself have never purchased any of these services, you must realize that there are people out there who do these services for others for a living. Likewise, in restaurants where tipping is customary, you are expected to compensate them for catering to you, so allow yourself to be catered to.

With the recent emergence of no-tipping establishments, it's actually even more reasonable to allow people to take care of you, as the living wages for those people have already been factored into the cost of everything you purchase in your visit. This is not to say you are incapable of helping yourself under normal circumstances, but while you are in a restaurant, there should be a mutual expectation that others will provide service for you so you can relax and enjoy some time by yourself or with others you presumably care for. Please enjoy leaving the heavy lifting to us.

Thirdly, but by no means least important, there is a safety issue that comes into play. A busy restaurant is like an intricate dance performed by a very well-rehearsed cast over perilous terrain. Imagine a Cirque de Soleil performance that revolves around a seated audience and then one audience member gets up and decides that he or she is a part of the performance. Granted, the cast may be able to dance around them, but if they slip and fall, it may cancel the performance for future guests, and for current guests, they get to see someone bumbling around and messing up the performance they also paid money to enjoy correctly.

This may seem like an overexaggeration, and admittedly to some extent, it is. If you are at a table with no silverware, and you are in current need of silverware to enjoy your food, no one is going to freak out if you get some from a nearby unoccupied table, at least not too much (someone else *is* supposed to be catering to *your* needs, after all). However, behind the bar, in the kitchen, and into the server area or drink well (where servers are passed drinks for their tables) are all places you should politely and kindly stay out of, not only for safety reasons but also to ensure that things continue to operate smoothly. Tying in to the last section, simply communicate what you need to someone, and he or she will get it for you—unless of course what you need is the bathroom. We're not monsters; we won't stop you.

5 c

DON'T TELL US HOW TO DO OUR JOBS, OR YOUR HELPING ISN'T HELPING

Think of your job and how much you would appreciate someone coming in off the street and telling you how to do it better, especially if it's a person who works in a completely different field from you. You don't need that kind of advice, and we don't need you to tell us how to do our jobs either. This is a sore spot for so many of us, and there's really no delicate way to put it. This ranges from actually telling us we are doing something wrong (a way you don't think it should be done) to grabbing plates from us (which could result in said plate spilling all over you) to walking back into the drink well or server station or kitchen (*get out*) to follow up or clarify something.

Remember all restaurants are different, and unless you run the one you are currently in, there is no reason for you to be making demands and ordering people about. Sit down and focus on enjoying the meal, and let us worry about how we're doing our jobs.

The one exception to this rule is when someone comes to your table with food, and you already have the table full or cluttered. It's perfectly OK for you to move things into a better location or temporarily hold on to an empty plate so we can set fresh food in front of you.

However, please resist the urge to stack up dishes for your server. You may think you're being helpful, but the way you stack them could prove perilous once they are moved, and a stack of dirty plates on a table sends a message that service is inattentive and dirty. This is actually something we can be guilty of when we go out to eat as well, since we are so used to doing it ourselves. Of everything else, this is not nearly as offensive, and most servers probably won't mind. Still, it's worth mentioning because this is something your server or his or her busser is being paid to do.

5D-1

DON'T EXPAND YOUR PERSONAL SPACE/TIME, OR TABLE SELECTION AND YOU!

By now, most of you may have noticed a trend in the reasons we ask you to not do things, and this one is no different: it is a matter of being polite to the other guests and participating in the safety of everyone around you as well as yourself.

First, let's discuss general spreading out, as this is partially a consideration to the restaurant and partially to other guests. On the restaurant side, some places depend on packing as many people into their space as possible while still providing an expected level of service. For that reason, their walkways are wide enough, but barely. If you need additional space, request a booth if they are available, or try to visit during off-peak hours. If people are brushing up against you every time they pass by, you are probably sitting out too far.

The next thing to consider is table space and the time you spend at that table. First, for you business folks: we all understand sometimes a table for two is not big enough to hold all the things you want to eat, plus your laptop, plus all the documents you need to look over, and for the most part, we don't mind that you are using it as an impromptu conference room— as long as you are mindful of our business hours and our peak time periods and compensate your server accordingly for the additional time you're there (which often means that he or she needs to stay there longer as well).

So if noon to 2:00 p.m. is the only time you have for your business meeting, you may want to order something to go or for delivery, or find an out-of-the-way place that doesn't fill up with other people during its lunch periods. Generally speaking, if we can accommodate your request, we will, but our business is as dependent on putting as many butts in as many seats as we can, when we can, as yours is on landing that contract, or whatever it is you normal people do. Besides, who wants to have a conversation when you're in a room where everyone is talking over each other?

On the opposite side of the spectrum are the casual diners. You may have the entire day free and want to spend three or four hours catching up with an old friend with a light lunch. Again, that is perfectly fine, but please pay attention to your surroundings and your location. If the place is filled to the brim and is known to be busy, it would probably be best to finish your meals and then go for a walk or do something else, because odds are there are other people who want to eat as well and only have a limited time to do so during that time period. In the span of those three to four hours, your server could have easily attended two to four more groups of people at that table. Imagine you were one of those people in those waiting groups.

Again, there are options, and by no means are we saying that you are forbidden to do so (except at some places where they actually do have time limits on how long you can be there). The best option as mentioned previously would be finding a place that was less busy or come near the end of their lunch (and leaving when it starts to fill for dinner). As a general rule of thumb, take a quick glance every once in a while; if you don't see any empty tables around you, there are probably other people waiting, and you shouldn't take forty-five minutes to finish that one slice of cake between the two of you.

If it's empty, by all means knock yourself out, as long as the restaurant is still open for business and you remember to compensate your server for sticking around to refill your water or the busser who needs to clean your table before he or she leaves for the day. Also be aware that you may be transferred from one server to another depending on their shifts. If this happens, the person may inform you he or she is leaving and ask if you would like to close out with him or her or transfer your current tab to a new server. Either option is fine, but it is more courteous to close out with the departing server since restaurants usually tip out their coworkers based on their sales. More on that later.

Both of these situations are specifically focused on one to four people; again, if your group is larger than that, make a phone call ahead of time and talk to a manager about accommodating your group. He or she may be able to work something out, or it may become obvious you should probably find another place that fits your time and budget constraints. There aren't many who will openly turn away your business, but every location has its own policies and capacities, and even though they may be perfect for another dining situation, there are some places that are better suited for your current one.

Now that that matter is out of the way, we can discuss the actual table you want to sit at. Assuming you didn't seat yourself and that you most assuredly didn't get seated at a dirty table (please, please say something to someone if you did get seated at a dirty table. Don't even sit down if you see it right away; no one in their right mind is going to hold it against you), you may be taken to your table by a host or server or manager. If you have made a reservation beforehand (go you!), you may have preselected a booth, a table, a specific table in the restaurant, a specific server's section (those last two predicated on you having been to the restaurant before), or any combination thereof.

If you didn't make a reservation, no worries. You will be taken to a suitable table for you, as deemed by the server rotation. If you see a specific spot that you would like to sit in, mention it as early as possible. If you want a booth or a regular table, if you want to sit by a window or a specific feature, all that should be communicated before being led to your table. The staff will be more than happy to accommodate you, but a longer wait time may be required.

The reason for this is that most restaurants are broken down into assigned server sections, and the seating is done on rotation through these sections to allow the server enough time between greeting one table and the next, being able to take and deliver orders without having other guests needing to be attended to at the same time. It is a very intricate game of time management. Depending on the service level, the server's individual approach, and his or her overall ability, some servers can take four to five tables being sat at once before needing a pause, while others may get overwhelmed at two because they spend more time at each individual table.

The person seating you usually knows which server on the floor is which. He or she knows whose section is ready to be sat and how to balance out seating so everyone has the opportunity to provide the very best service he or she can. Server sections are an invisible jigsaw puzzle that overlays the entire floor, and sometimes requesting a table right next to the one you were led to may belong to an entirely different server than the one you were intended to receive. This server may be occupied with other guests and not be able to provide you with the attention you deserve.

Eight times out of ten, we will do our very best to accommodate you, but please ask politely, and don't get offended if the answer is no—for instance, if there are two people in your party and you want to sit at a table for four. Depending on reservations, total seating capacity, level of current business, and restaurant policy, all these things are factored in consideration before giving you a yes or no answer.

If you sit in a spot, regardless of whether you sat yourself, please don't move yourself to another spot, as that spot may be reserved for another group of people. Even though you may not see them now, those people may have made special plans for that evening a very long time ago, and you may be throwing a very large wrench into those plans. Imagine you made dinner reservations for your grandmother's seventy-fifth birthday a month in advance at her favorite place, but when you got there with your family, you had to stand around and wait because two people had decided the table meant for you was really meant for them. Sorry, Grandma! Those people are jerks; don't be those people.

Another reason it's best not to change tables is because not only might you go from one server section to another, but also if you order food at one table and move without communicating to your server, your food may get delivered to the table you left if other people sit there shortly after you leave. The restaurant is not the wild savannah, and no one wants to have to hunt you down.

All that being said, if you are refused a spot, realize that it is not personal and it's done with a heavy heart. Believe me—we want your business, and we want to provide you with the very best service we can, but we have to be considerate to those who were considerate with us and made a sign of good faith by booking in advance.

Sometimes you may see a mostly empty restaurant but still cannot be seated—it's not about you; it's about the people who will be coming in after you. We don't know how long you will take by looking at you; we don't want to tell someone else they need to wait just like we don't want to tell you that you have to finish up and leave so someone else can have your spot. Sometimes, if it's early enough, we will seat you in a spot but inform you we have a reservation at the table an hour and a half or two hours from that time, so it can be under good faith that you will be finished by the time that party arrives. But again, this is completely dependent on which restaurant you walk into.

5D-2

DON'T EXPAND YOUR PERSONAL SPACE/TIME, OR STOP FLAILING ABOUT, LITERALLY AND METAPHORICALLY!

So by now you are definitely seated. Hooray! Time to relax and enjoy the company of others and/ or a great meal and a great dining experience. Around this time you will meet your server, who is there to cater not only to your needs but also to the needs of others around you. Some may think that only their needs matter or that their needs somehow should be top priority. Fortunately, with the aid of this book, you are able to be rational and considerate, and you realize all other guests have equal importance and that your server deserves that same respect. Your server should be pretty well versed on prioritizing his or her time and attention in his or her section and be able to interact with you to the level you need.

Once you are seated, please get comfortable, but also prepare to order! If you are with a group of people, this is especially important as some of those people may really be hungry. Take as much time as you need to decide, or if you're stuck, ask the server for some help, but you're in a restaurant to eat, right? Socializing is best done after your order is placed.

There are few things more frustrating than people who will sit around and talk for half an hour before even looking at the menu. If you do so, your server may not immediately be around when you *are* finally ready to order. If you send him or her away four times because you didn't want to look at the menu, no one is going to feel bad because you waited fifteen minutes before he or she came around when you *were* finally ready. Be considerate to the business, the people who work there, and the people who actually come in to eat immediately—don't dillydally about placing your order.

Since we have already gone over being literate, you have already saved both you and your server a *ton* of time because you know how to read a menu. If you have specific questions about something you can't figure out on the menu, need to explain an allergy, or would like your server's opinion between two or three dishes that all look like you would enjoy them, by all means ask. I myself am guilty of sometimes taking ten minutes to decide, even when I eat at the place I work. But when you are seated, the menu should be your top priority.

As a bit of a side note, let's be considerate of the menu for a bit. How much "customization" does it allow? Some places may let you mix and match to your dear sweet heart's content; others may only have five to seven entree choices listed, and that's it. Since you may have looked at it before seating, either online or at the door, you should have a good idea of what you're getting into before you sit down. The menu is essentially the playbook for the restaurant. Some places are like a sandbox; others are a bit more direct and formal. These second types usually have an executive chef, and the menu is their expression of food. It's important to look and discern which one is which and which one you're actually in the mood for.

I say this not to be mean, but to convey a very simple message. If you want only the things you know you like in a way that you like them, that's great; it really is. If it's on the menu, do it. However, if you're feeling a bit more adventurous and willing to go outside of the comfortable, just take the dish as-is. If you have a food **allergy**, inform your server; see if the dish can be made without that item or if there is something that would be more suitable for your needs. If you have a food **aversion**, you can still ask if the dish can be made without it if you really want the rest of the dish, or you can order something else.

If the menu doesn't specifically mention food modifications, however, please don't create your own menu item. Just because you see item "a" has ingredient "x" and item "b" has ingredient "y" (sorry for the algebra) doesn't mean you get to play Iron Chef. A slight exception is asking if they have something, if you don't see it on the menu. If you've been there before and the menu item you loved is gone, they may still be able to make it. On the other hand, if you're in a Chinese restaurant, don't ask if they have spaetzle. Not only is the answer most likely no, but the people you're with may question if you're fit to be outside without a safety helmet. Again, if you're at a place with a set menu, you're there to experience certain flavor combinations, not to make them up yourself.

As a personal example, growing up, I *hated* brussels sprouts. You could not get me to eat them, but as I got older, I finally gave them another try, and they were delicious! It turned out my mom just didn't know how to prepare them properly (sorry, Mom), but if I hadn't tried them prepared by someone else, I would have never known how truly amazing those little cruciferous veggies could be.

The point is, you may have had something done one way a dozen times, but if someone else does it another way, it could completely change the way you feel about the dish or the ingredient. If you haven't had that restaurant's dish before, how do you know you need to alter it? Do you know more about that dish than the person who created it? It's a bit presumptuous to think so. If you want something the same way you expect it, do it yourself, or go to where you've had it and liked it before; otherwise, break out of your box and give it a chance. (All we are saying is give peas a chance! [Sorry, couldn't help it.])

So once your order is placed, you've got some time before the food shows up. Feel free to strike up a conversation with your group, but be mindful of the type of establishment you are in. If you're in a high-class joint, as a consideration to the other guests, don't be the loudest group in the room. If you're in a place where language might be an issue, watch your mouth. Not to say that you can't say what you want; just don't bellow it out if there are kids nearby. Also, keep in mind that most guests who didn't come in with you may not want to be part of your conversation, so please don't try to include them in it.

Like your words should not be going all over the place, please make sure your hands are not going all over the place. This is not limited to just not touching the staff inappropriately; remember, in most restaurants there is limited space, and people may be moving quickly through it with extremely hot or extremely cold things. Throwing your arms out for emphasis on whatever you're speaking about may just hit a tray and spill said hot or cold things on the server, on another guest, or even yourself. You're not performing in a theater; tone it down.

So after a bit of conversation in which you're in control of your personal space, your food finally arrives—or does it? If you are a single diner, it shouldn't be that hard to tell if your order is complete, but when large tables are getting their food, there is the potential for things to fall through the cracks, especially when it gets busy. Nobody's happy about it, but it does happen from time to time. To counter it as best we can, most servers will announce each dish they are setting on the table, not just as a way to ensure you got what you ordered but for you to see and hear what the dish actually looks like at the same time.

Sometimes, there is so much that either multiple servers or multiple trips from the kitchen may be necessary. If you don't get your food right away, don't immediately assume they have forgotten it, as they should be making sure everyone has something in front of them. But if you get something you know for sure you didn't order, inform them immediately of the error, before they leave the table or before they even set the dish down if possible, as that may have been intended for some other guest entirely.

Once the server believes your order to be complete, he or she will usually enquire with you to make sure you agree by asking, "Is there anything else you need at the moment?" or something along those lines. Please consider this carefully; take a few seconds to take everything in, and note everything you can think of that may be missing. If not, wonderful, we hope you enjoy your meal.

However, if you do notice something and mention it, again please make sure you've identified everything.

There are some people who will continue to ask for one more thing, then get that thing, then ask for one *more* thing, then get that thing, then ask for one *more* thing, until the server has made multiple return visits that should have only required one.

Imagine that this is some other group of people (because now you know better), and you are watching this happen because you need a refill on your drink or your bill, and the server can't break away from those guests to tend to you. Your server will most likely apologize for the delay, but there is little he or she could have done in that situation, as most restaurants have an emphatic priority structure on food delivery time. Besides that, sometimes weird things just happen.

Hopefully, the restaurant staff works as a cohesive team to counter this, and a manager or another server will notice the gap and fill in. But when it's busy everywhere, there's not much that can be done other than to offer our sincere apologies when we can finally get to you. And we are sorry, because those people are flailing about mentally and can't focus on communicating their needs concisely. Jerks.

5D-3

DON'T EXPAND YOUR PERSONAL SPACE/TIME COMMUNALLY, OR PLEASE KEEP YOUR DOGS AND CHILDREN LEASHED AT ALL TIMES

Being a parent can be rough. (Maybe—I don't know, personally.) But being a decent person shouldn't be. If the place you are eating at has a designated play area for children, by all means kick your feet up and let the children play for a bit while still keeping an eye on them. If they need to go for a walk because you've been sitting in one spot too long, by all means take them on a walk, supervised.

However, it's very important to remember that if you really want the best for your little demon spawn, restaurants can be pretty dangerous places. If something is not a toy, don't let your kid play with it. If they want to move, you need to move with them to make sure they don't get hit or fall or run out the door into traffic.

Obviously, we have no intention of telling you how to raise your children, but you need to be respectful of the other guests around you, who probably don't want to hear a screaming infant for ten minutes because you're just too tired to deal with it. Those people might not tell you either, but they are judging you as hard as they can. Deal with it. Take that screaming monster outside, and do whatever you need to however you need to do it. If you really don't want to deal with your child anymore, I hear shaking them helps. You are a bad parent and shouldn't have procreated.

Whoa...that got a little dark there for a little second, so let's bring it back. Let's say you don't have kids, or you do and are managing them well, but you see a friend or coworker in the same restaurant and want to say hi. Waves are good. Brief hellos are fine too. If there is space at the table to merge parties, by all means merge parties. However, please don't stand around for more than a minute having a full-blown conversation.

As mentioned earlier, you're not helping anyone by clogging up the pathways; you're actually posing a huge risk and a huge inconvenience for everyone. Arrange for a later meeting if there's anything a simple hey cannot contain, and find your seat.

5 E

DON'T ACCEPT WHAT YOU DON'T WANT

nother venture into what should be common sense, but let's go into it, shall we? As mentioned previously, if your server has a dish you didn't order, tell him or her immediately. Not only could it have been for someone else, but if you eat a thing, the expectation is that you pay for a thing. We are in a service industry, and as with most services, payment comes after completion of the task.

You can't go to a concert or a basketball game and then decide whether you want to pay. If you have someone mow your lawn and you decide you didn't like the way your lawn was mowed and that you don't have to pay him or her for it, you could get into some legal trouble. I've never been a member of law enforcement, but I'm fairly sure that if you call the cops and tell them you don't want to pay for something you took, they won't be siding with you.

However, we have such a strong desire to make you happy that we incur these losses on an almost daily basis. If the first half of our game sucked, we may only charge you for the second. If you don't like our landscaping, we will start it over again and only charge you for the end results. This is, point of fact, a pretty sweet deal, but it's one that less scrupulous people often take advantage of.

Why do we do it? Because you only have so much space in your belly and we want you to be **completely satisfied** with how you fill it. If you eat half of a thing you didn't want, or something you wanted but it didn't taste right or was undercooked or whatever, that is space in your belly that neither of us can get back during your visit. If you fill up on something you hated, and send it away because you don't want to finish it or have anything else, it is a loss for all of us. We lose money and the opportunity to impress you; you have a crappy meal, so no one is happy. Why do this to yourself?

Don't.

If the dish isn't to your liking, send it back as soon as you notice it. We will remake it or get you something else; it's not going to hurt our feelings. You do not need to suffer in silence because you don't want to cause a fuss or maybe the dish will get better if you keep on eating it. It won't. Send it back until we bring you something you're happy to be eating. If nothing we have makes you happy, we are sorry. We are so sorry, but we need the opportunity to get it right for you.

With all this in mind, remember to please be mindful of where you are eating, not only the location of the restaurant, but the type of restaurant it is. You shouldn't expect a diner to provide you with anything more than diner food. On the opposite end of the spectrum, if you are paying fifty dollars plus for a steak, it had better be the exact temperature you asked it to be. Unless it's over medium-well, in which case you are a savage. I'm not sure who taught you to read, but he or she is a regular Jane Goodall; I'm honestly surprised you've made it this far into the book without trying to eat it. Insulted? Now is a good time to go on to…

5F

DON'T DEMEAN, OBJECTIFY, OR
BELITTLE THE PEOPLE WHO ARE
TRYING TO BE NICE TO YOU, OR
HOW TO COMMUNICATE LIKE A
CIVILIZED HUMAN BEING

I will apologize in advance for not fluffing this up a bit; the next part is going to be very direct because really, the whole book can be boiled down to this: You are a guest. You can range anywhere from an honored guest to a tolerated guest, but you will always be a guest, not some feudal lord who can just barge in and have his way with the place and the people who work there. You are visiting a place that is not yours, being maintained by hardworking people who also **do not belong to you**. Please remember this at all times, and treat them at least with the respect you should be giving to any productive member of our society, because that's what civilization is.

Now, with that unpleasantness out of the way, let's go over some common ways to not be a jerk. These can all be applied to your everyday life, not just when you are visiting a restaurant.

Don't take your crappy day/life out on other people (a.k.a. the Golden Rule.). We all have bad days and times when we are less than our best selves; we understand. But if you find yourself taking out your frustration on someone who is just trying to help you, maybe you shouldn't be going out into public. Assuming it's already too late at this point, just try to remember that it's a mark of true character when, and I may be paraphrasing here, you realize that other people may have just as much shit going on in their lives, but at least they have the decency to keep it to themselves. If you can't say something nice, save it for the people who know you well enough that your negativity won't bother them. Fun fact: Some hippy study somewhere has proved if you're nicer to other people when you're feeling bad, you will eventually feel better yourself.

Acknowledge when you are spoken to, and the context of said speech. When someone says hello to you, it's polite to acknowledge him or her. A simple hi is fine or you could even go to the lengths of "and a very good day to you as well, sir/madam!" Even just a nod and some eye contact if you don't like to talk or are engaged in something else like a phone call. Greetings are a pretty common thing in our field, and we all pretty much have to say hi to you if you get within five feet of us. It's a thing; I promise.

It's also a little insulting when someone ignores this mandatory greeting. Imagine saying hi to a friend you see walking down the street, and he or she just keeps going like he or she doesn't even see you. Even if you're caught up in what you're doing, always be aware that there are other people around you, and they may be trying to talk to you. Likewise, what they're saying may be important for you to know. When someone inquires to your well-being, your response should be reflective of your well-being. Let's compare two ways of responding to the question "How are you tonight?"

Response 1: Diet Coke.

Response 2: I'm all right, a little parched, though. I would be a lot better if I had a Diet Coke!

Notice both responses communicate the need for a refreshing soda. The difference is, response one is coming from someone who has no people skills and maybe doesn't realize he or she is being a dick. Formalities waste a bit of time; yes it's true, but if a stranger comes up to you and says, "What do you want?" most people would be a little insulted. It's like that whole "being an adult" thing, where if someone asks you how you are, you have to say, "I'm fine," even if everything hurts and you're dying. Acknowledge that a question has been asked and give a correct response to prove you are aware of your surroundings.

Don't expect your server to be clairvoyant. When you are first introduced to your server, be aware he or she might not know everything going on in your life. If you're eating on borrowed time, let your server know if you've got a show you need to be at in an hour. (The exception would be if you are eating at an airport, it's safe to presume the person knows you have a plane to catch.) It's also especially important to let the server know ahead of time if your group wants separate checks or if you're under a time crunch. This can save precious minutes at the end of your meal because usually bills for large groups get run in all together, and if they don't know they need to keep track of who had what, your whole group and your server will be frustrated when you needed to be out the door five minutes ago but your one bill needed to be broken into thirty individual tickets. If you let the person know what's going on to start with, he or she can make it work for you. If not, remember people only know what's going on once you tell them and be patient.

Say "please" and "thank you." This is huge; manners in general are huge. When you are asking for something, include "please" every time. When you are receiving something or acknowledging an inquiry, include "thank you" every time. You may or may not be amazed at how well this goes over with your server (or anyone else you ever talk to. Again, please don't feel you have to limit this behavior to inside a restaurant.

Life skill!). Even and especially if you are being a complete pain in the butt, this will help you out immensely.

Don't interrupt when someone is speaking to you. Yes, we can be guilty of this too, but if you're in the middle of a story and everyone else is waiting to order drinks, your server will find a time between your breaths to address the table. If you see your server standing there quietly, by all means get to a stopping point where you can pick up later and give the server your attention. He or she may have to tell you about the specials of the day regardless of whether you know what you want or not. If you cut someone off midsentence, not only is it rude but it could break his or her train of thought. Mostly, though, it's just rude. Why are you being rude to someone who is trying to take care of you? This is not the way you should be behaving.

Don't. Snap. Your Fingers. At Someone Else. Ever. This carries across to whistling like you're calling a dog, yelling your bartender's name out across a crowded bar, or calling someone "sugar tits," "sweetie," or "hey, you." Are you getting the picture here? There is not enough space in this book to list all the insulting ways you can address another human being. I implore you—think of every single one you can, and then do not use any of them.

If you do not know the person you are speaking to well enough, refer to him or her as "ma'am" or "madam" if the person is a lady or "sir" if it's a guy. Eye contact is usually enough to get most wait staff's attention, and you can throw in a wave if you're feeling energetic. "Excuse me" can work if you're close enough that you can say it using your inside voice and be heard.

If you need something, please be respectful to the person you need to get that thing for you. If he or she can't get to you right away, wait. If he or she saw you, the person will get to you when he or she can, or send someone else to you. **Be patient**.

No Touching. Unless you know the person well enough for a hug or a handshake, there is absolutely no reason for you touch or grab anyone else. Even a tap on the shoulder could be taking things too far depending on context. If a server needs to touch your arm to get your attention, don't presume that this is giving you the liberty to touch whomever wherever you want. By all means, take this little nugget of thought with you no matter where you go. People will despise you substantially less than they probably currently do. Personal space is personal.

5 G

DON'T MAKE MESSES ON PURPOSE, OR YOU ARE NOT OUR DECORATOR

Sometimes food jumps out of your plate, off your fork, or even out of your mouth. Crumbs just can't be helped, and there will be the inevitable parents bringing in Cheerios for their toddler to basically play with, and eventually all ends up crushed on the floor. We get that; we accept it.

What we don't get is why a grown-ass adult would squeeze out an entire bottle of ketchup onto his or her plate and then layer napkins on top of it. Or shred toilet paper and seat covers all over a bathroom. This is first and foremost an inconvenience to the other guests who show up after you; how many times have you walked into a bathroom with a terrible need to take a sit and discovered the only toilet paper to be found is ground up on the floor? In this day and age, we are becoming more and more aware of the finite resources on the planet, so don't waste things other people need to use. Also, don't take things that can be reused. I'm sure these thoughts must be coming as a shock to some people, but theft is actually a bad thing.

If you are dissatisfied with something, use your words. Don't throw a silent temper tantrum. If you're bored, try sparking a conversation with the people in your group or your server or bartender; it could turn out a lot better than the jelly and creamer sculpture that no one else will enjoy.

Also, please resist the urge to redecorate. If you see a potted plant in a spot, it's not up to you to decide where it would look better. The same thing goes for pictures, statues, displays, tables, chairs, or anything not bolted down, really. If it's not yours, leave it alone.

This takes a new level of importance when factoring in tables. **Don't move the tables.** For one, you could hurt yourself; even if you're used to lifting heavier objects, tables are awkward to move. Secondly, by moving that table, you could be clogging the layout of the dining room and impeding service to everyone just because you had a friend join you later on in your meal. Thirdly, remember that we are here to do the heavy lifting. You should not pay to strain yourself. This is why it's important to communicate your needs to the wait staff; they will either join a table to yours properly or move you and your party to a larger table. Everyone wins. You get to continue to relax and your server will appreciate your consideration involving him or her in your needs.

5H-1

DON'T FORGET THAT PEOPLE ARE WORKING AND NEED TO BE PAID

This is the sorest of all points and one most people in our industry shy away from. Discussing payment and gratuity is not something most people relish having to mention to our guests. The subject is taboo to the extent that I could face a potential blacklisting from my industry if this whole thing goes south. However, it would be remiss of me to leave this out if I really intended to include **all** the information you **need** to know, so hopefully one day I will be forgiven.

There are an increasing number of places now that have removed tips from the equation. Make sure you know if the place you are eating is one of those places. You are still paying for services rendered at these places; it's just being applied directly to the cost of every item there. Directly or indirectly, the wait staff is dependent on your dollar for their paychecks.

If you are at a location that still relies on tips, the standard is 20 percent of the original total. If you feel you've received abysmal service and were neglected despite attempting to communicate your needs, that percentage can dip as low as 15 percent, any lower, and you're basically saying you don't ever intend to go back there. On the opposite end of the spectrum, if you received service that went above and beyond what you should realistically expect from an experience dining out (which, now that you have this book you know what that entails), it's completely acceptable to throw a little extra on there just as a thank-you.

If you need some clarification on what that extra entails, I will take this time to remind you ever so politely that the wait staffs are not professional photographers, tour guides, counselors, or babysitters. Having a server guide you through a wine list is one thing; expecting them to guide your experience through the town is quite another. Again, all restaurants are different, so some places might sing "Happy Birthday" for you; others may just bring out a complimentary dessert with a candle in it—for those sort of things, it's best to ask in advance.

If you really liked the server, get his or her name for the next time as well. In our industry, having repeat guests ask for a server specifically says a lot about how well the person does his or her job, and having a guaranteed group of people who know how to dine out (thanks to this book and common decency, yay!) is one of the greatest reliefs a server can hope for during a busy shift. I digress.

The reason for that 20 percent is that you are paying for service. Though the server is your main point of contact, there are other people contributing who also need to get paid and do so through a percentage of your server's tips or total sales. These people are the hosts, bussers, bartenders, even the kitchen sometimes, and usually a server will only walk, or finish his or her shifts with about 75 percent of his or her tips, more or less.

If you leave the server 5 percent of your bill, he or she will most likely be paying that all to someone else. If you stiff him or her (leave nothing), you are effectively costing the person money to work. Imagine if you had to pay an hour's worth of your wages every day to your boss just to work for him or her; how happy would you be with that situation? How welcome would someone who asked that of you be if he or she came over to your house next week? The food and drink prices are as low as they can be in these places because even though tipping is technically optional—but so is washing your hands before you eat.

Please keep in mind that service can be affected by a myriad of things: food and drinks being prepared improperly, business level, overall cleanliness, and so forth. However, your server has little to no control over most of that. Instead ask yourself, was he or she attentive? Did he or she address and/or correct any issue I brought to his or her attention? Was he or she accommodating to my needs? Did he or she communicate with me when an issue came up on his or her end? The server is the messenger of the restaurant; please don't shoot him or her.

5H-2

DON'T BE UNGRATEFUL

If something is given to you on the house, or complimentary, thank whomever gave it to you and tip as if you had ordered it on top of the original bill. If you are given something once, treat it like an unexpected gift from a friend, and don't expect it every time. You would probably think this would be common knowledge, but here it is, getting its own special focus.

Usually, you will be informed that these items are being gifted to you. If someone sets down an order of fries and you didn't order them, make sure the person who set the dish down is aware that you didn't order them. If it was given to you by accident and you ate it anyway, you may be expected to pay for that item.

This is closely related to tipping—keep in mind that telling someone he or she did a great job does not cover his or her living expenses. Saying what a wonderful time you had and leaving 10 percent of a discounted total is just as bad as spitting in someone's face, and ultimately it's your money that is your voice. Hooray capitalism!

51

DON'T STAY PAST YOUR WELCOME, OR MANAGE YOUR TIME EFFECTIVELY

This is almost as sensitive a subject as tipping, but as mentioned previously, time is money. The unfiltered truth is that the smaller the group is and the less expensive the bill, the more important it is to know when it's time to leave. For casual places a couple should only take about forty-five minutes from start to finish; for fine dining the same two should only need about an hour and a half max. This is not to say you will be kicked out after that time (unless it's made clear to you that could happen). If you think you'll be staying longer, communicate it to the restaurant as soon as possible. Knowing your timeframe helps not only you to plan your day or evening but the restaurant to plan its day as well. Here are some helpful hints to get what you need in the time-frame you've got.

Coordinate your times with the other members of your party. Some places won't even seat you until your entire party has arrived. If they do, there shouldn't be more than ten to fifteen minutes to wait till the rest of your group shows up. If by that time they aren't there, tell yourself they're not coming and eat, because you are preventing other people who are there from using that table and wanting to eat. This ties back to peak hours of your dining establishment. If you have friends who are notoriously half an hour or forty-five minutes late to everything, make sure you plan on a place that will accommodate you when it is not filled to the brim.

Once you're seated, look at the menu and don't put it down until you know what you want to order. If you're having trouble, ask your server for help. Reference the menu section in the "being literate" section of this book for more details.

Put your phone away. *Put It Away.* If you're by yourself, it's completely OK if you have it out after you order and until your food arrives. If you are with a group, however, have a conversation with an actual human being, or find a new group of people you actually enjoy talking to. Eating is one of the most social times of the day and one that is deeply ingrained into society. When your phone is out, so are you. If you want to snap a quick picture of your food before you eat it, no one will mind as long as you don't turn it into a full-blown photo shoot. Otherwise, keep your electronic tether out of the conversation as much as possible. You may be surprised how nice it is to actually engage people directly.

If you can't eat anymore, get a box or put your napkin on the plate to show you are done with it. Some people take longer to eat than others. We get it, and we don't want to rush you. But if you're idly just pushing food around on your plate, either have it wrapped up or taken away so we know you're done eating.

Once you are done eating, you need to be done sitting. Life is short. We understand the importance of catching up and connecting with people you care about, but we want to do that stuff too, and so do other guests. Enjoy your meal, dessert, and coffee, but when you're not ordering any more, it's time to finish up and find another activity to share with each other. Your server will not say this to you, but as a decent human being considerate to others, you should know it.

If you are the last ones in the entire restaurant, or if it's past the restaurant's stated close time, you need to leave ASAP. Sometimes you get to a place five to ten minutes before it closes. It happens, and people will be a little ruffled about it, but there are ways to mitigate the damage and still have a pleasant experience. Apologize for the late arrival, state your awareness of the closing time, order, and finish your meal as quickly as possible. It's polite, and it's the best you can do in your circumstances.

If it's 10:15 p.m. and the restaurant closed at 10:00 p.m. but there's still another table or a few tables occupied, don't feel rushed, but also realize that you can't be held accountable for those other people. You still should be polite and finish as soon as comfortably possible. If you really want to endear yourself to the staff, thank them for letting you stay as you leave so other guests will get the hint. You rock!

SECTION 6

THINGS YOU SHOULD AVOID
SAYING IN A RESTAURANT

All right! We made it through the *ate*s! Well, now we're going to incorporate them all and finish up with some fun little phrases that we in restaurants get to hear a little too often, why you probably shouldn't say them, and maybe an alternative recommendation. I realize that for some evil people out there, this could be filling out their arsenal completely, but I am presuming that you are fortunately not one of those people.

You'll also probably notice quite a few of these have been mentioned already; think of this as a quick reference guide for the rest of the book once you have read your way through and enjoy.

Are you open? Usually, if you can walk through the doors, we're open. We may not have any guests, but if the hours say we're open, yes, we are open.

Do you have (item not listed on menu), or Could you make me (item not listed on the menu)? No. If we did, it would be on the menu. The exception of course, are those delightful secret menus, if you've been there before and a menu item is not listed any longer, they may still be able to make it for you. Still it's best to prepare for a no.

Is (menu item or ingredient) gluten-free? This is the bane of many servers' existence because the gluten-free crowd is the least knowledgeable of their "condition" than any other food aversion out there. A person with a shellfish allergy knows the lobster bisque is out of the question. A person with a wheat allergy wouldn't walk within ten feet of a bakery. A person who is gluten-free usually ends up asking if potatoes are gluten-free (they are, by the way, but the fryer oil they're being dunked in to make french fries probably isn't, which is something you would definitely know if you had celiac disease). Instead of asking about individual items, if it's really a big deal, go for the whole scope by saying truthfully, "I'm choosing not to eat gluten; what can I have?" You will probably get a very concise list of everything you can choose from—I promise.

Are there any other good restaurants around here? You're asking us to recommend our competition to you when you're in our doors? No, we are the only one in existence. We can probably mention some fun things to do that are not restaurant related, but when we are working at a place, that is the only place we know, and the only place we are worried about.

What's good here? Everything. Look at the menu. Do you see something that looks appetizing? Order that. See something you don't think would be good? Stay away from that, but realize other people like it because otherwise, it wouldn't sell, and we'd take it off the menu. If it wasn't good, it wouldn't be on the menu. If it was bad and on the menu, the restaurant would probably go out of business pretty quick. Have you ever overheard someone say, "Hey, let's stop in here; I hear they have a really disgusting pork chop that no one can finish because it's so awful!" Seems a bit silly, doesn't it? Better questions would be more specific, like "Which dishes are you known for?" or "What is the most ordered item on the menu?" or "What's your favorite thing here?" is also good, but can sometimes be the most expensive dish on the menu, because check averages and sometimes it really is the best thing on the menu.

Is the owner around? Or I know (owner's name); (are they) here? Usually, no. If they are, though, and they know you, they'll come by and say hi. No one is impressed that you know the owner, because we probably know them too. Usually these people who ask have no idea who the owner is but know his or her name and are expecting complimentary items or to meet a celebrity and will even ask when the owner is in clear view. Your service will not be any better if you say this. We will not give you things for free for knowing a name. If you know the owner that well, give him or her a call and find out where he or she is.

Can we add (x) more people? As mentioned previously in this book, this one is semitricky, because if it's one or two or on a slow night, maybe. If it's four or more during peak times, most likely no. If it's already packed, then definitely no; they will either have to sit at a different table entirely or wait to be seated at a different table entirely depending on how many people are already in the building. Fire-code capacity will always trump you saving an extra seat for your buddies waiting outside in a line. You can meet up after dinner and talk about this book and how it helped you avoid situations like this.

I used to (or currently) work in a restaurant. This one can be a little tricky because it depends on the context in which it's used. If you're using it as a means of accepting an apology, such as if your server came over to tell you your food is taking a little longer, it can be a bit of a relief, because you get it. If you are using it because things aren't going your way and you would do things differently, then no, you did and do not. Again, the overarching theme of the book is showing compassion. It's what we do. And it's not just when we're working; it pervades every interaction we have in life. Consideration for others tends to be a hard habit to break. If you don't have that hardwired, you haven't worked in a restaurant, at least not long enough for it to matter.

So what do you really do? Or **You must not like your job.** What we really do is try to provide the best service we can to people of varying integrity, because some sick, twisted part of us actually wants to make other people happy. Just because we don't particularly care for some of the people we interact with does not mean we have any desire to go into any other career field. Don't presume to know anything about a person after talking to him or her for only five minutes. Trust me; the people who don't like the work we do don't last in our industry very long. Not too surprisingly, when you insult or question someone's passion, they usually don't respond well.

Yes, some people use the service industry to get themselves through college, but others prefer it as a career. Likewise, not everyone can mask their emotions, and some days are better than others. Hell, some hours are better than others. It's rude to presume you know what's going on inside someone else's head. Leave the psychoanalysis to the professionals (and the bartenders).

I tip well, or, **We'll take good care of you.** Historically proven, only bad tippers say this. On average, these are the 10–15 percent tippers, and as soon as we hear this line, it's over. If you are a good tipper (because you read this book, yay!), just leave a good tip befitting the service you received. Money talks, and talkers tip like shit.

Do you know who I am? Obviously not—or maybe we do, and it doesn't matter, because what we do know for sure is what you are acting like (hint: it's an asshole). We pride ourselves on providing consistent service to all our guests. If you are having a specific issue, communicate it as reasonably and politely as you can. You always catch more bees with honey.

I called ahead, or **I had a reservation (when you didn't).** Most places that require reservations take this *very* seriously, and if you don't know whom you spoke with, at what time on which day, they might not believe you. Especially if you say you called that morning and spoke to a guy when no men were working that morning, or if you say you were promised a reservation when no more were left months ago or no reservations were allowed that particular day. Because if you drop in with fifteen people and legitimately called to make a reservation and that person didn't log it or promised you something he or she shouldn't have, that person very well could lose his or her job. So yeah, it's pretty serious. You will not make friends with anyone by lying, so don't.

This isn't as good as (another restaurant or someone else's preparation). Then why are you here? Seriously, if that's what you wanted, why are you wasting your time with anything else? Did someone drag you here? If so, he or she probably doesn't care, and you should probably just keep that opinion to yourself. If it's not as good as the last time you had it at that location, of course by all means be specific and tell your server. Otherwise you're just being pretentious.

I'm on Yelp, or **I'm going to write a bad review.** We'll go over this in the last section. Again in context this might not be so bad, but 95 percent of the times we hear this is when a guest has a stick shoved up his or her ass or is trying to get things for free. Cool story; maybe you should reevaluate your life and figure out why dogging on other people is the only way you can get any satisfaction from it. You are the worst. Don't even say this to yourself unless you have followed my earlier advice and brought your problems to the attention of the staff. If you leave unhappy because we didn't know something was wrong, you only have yourself to blame.

We won't take long. We have no way of knowing what you consider "long," and usually, your idea of long and ours are completely different. So please excuse us for not seating you at a table that is reserved an hour from now. Those people might come early, or they might come late, but we've made a promise to them to have their table ready for them. If you are specific about your time expectations, we will accommodate you the best we can, but we won't risk upsetting someone who took the time and consideration that you did not.

The customer is always right. The customer is rarely right, but most of the time, we can accommodate this fallacy. If we are rejecting some notion you have, it is either because it's too far from what we can realistically do or (more likely) because you are just being monumentally rude. This phrase will not win over anybody. Yes, we have heard it, but odds are what you are asking for can't be done. Sorry.

Well done. Unless you're complimenting someone on his or her service or performance, or are pregnant and ordering a burger or some other sort of ground meat.

What do you mean (things) cost (money)? News flash: things cost money. Some places have tighter budgets than others. We are not trying to gouge you; we are informing you that if you want something, there will be a charge for it. If you are asking for clarification, maybe you should have bought an economics book instead of this light read. Some places will give you all the ranch you want without batting an eye, but it does not mean the place down the street won't charge you a buck for every ounce.

It was horrible. Used mostly after eating everything on a plate, usually as a joke. We've heard it a million times, and it's still not funny. If everything really was horrible, you should have mentioned it well before now. Even if you are an actual comedian, please don't make jokes about bad food or bad service.

You should smile more. Do people tell you to smile when you're cleaning out your rain gutters or writing code or whatever it is you do for a living? Of course not. Just because we enjoy our jobs doesn't mean there should be smiles plastered on our faces. (Although if we could wear masks that looked like big, creepy smiles…) Should we be pleasant? Yes. Does being pleasant mean smiling like an addle-headed ninny when we've got fifteen different things drawing our focus? Sorry, no, it does not. Also, realize sometimes a smile in a situation where you are pissed because your steak is taking half an hour to be ready is not the best physical response we can give to assure you we're taking the matter seriously.

There are probably tons more, but you get the idea. These are just the most common ones we hear. Notice phrases like "May I speak to your manager?" or "This isn't what I ordered!" are not included because by now, you should know that these phrases need to be used when you have a legitimate concern.

Section 7

Food Blogging and You, or To Yelp or Not to Yelp, That Is the Question

So you've made it through your entire dining experience. Hopefully, by following the recommendations laid out in this guide, you were able to have an amazing experience, and now you feel like you should tell someone about it. Well, not *someone* in particular, but the entire logical, compassionate, non-satirical Internet in general.

Now, I'm not going to explicitly say you should or should not write an online review. On the contrary, I feel that just by having this book in your possession makes you better qualified than at least half of the other people out there. However, not having my book does not prevent anyone with Internet access from writing, and because of this, you may find your target audience flooded with reviews by people whose heads may or may not be shoved up their own asses. So, you may need to find a way to differentiate yourself to stand out of the crowd.

If you are a professional food blogger, please tell your audience to read this book. If you're making a living off writing about food, you probably don't need the advice in this section. Keep in mind that I myself am not a food critic but more of a people critic. However, these are some things I would consider when writing a review.

Are you writing because you want to share your experience or because you want to prove how funny/ smart/cultured you are? The narration does tend to set the tone, so here are a few hints. Life is funny enough as it is. Usually the funniest things that happen are not jokes you can come up with, but the experience you had. Try to avoid throwing out one-liners and focus more on the experience to prove your point. Second, as we have established, there are quite a few places out there that take, shall we say, creative liberty with the names of classic dishes. If you notice it's prepared a little differently than how it traditionally is, chances are other people know about it too. Instead, focus on how those changes affect the dish; does it appeal more or less to your individual taste? Third, remember that the point of being cultured is having developed not only your education and tastes but also your manners. Try to avoid personal attacks on the wait staff and especially on the cooks, unless one of them did knowingly and intentionally insult you personally—it just makes you seem like a jerk. Of course, you already knew that.

Are you writing from an informed standpoint and are you being fair? Again, having this book sets you high and above most of those who have not read it, but let's break this down a bit. As an example, how often do you see reviews complaining about the price of something? As someone who is able to read a menu, the only time price should be mentioned is if you were overcharged the stated price; otherwise you will come off as being cheap. Instead, maybe focus on saying how the quality of what you received differs from another time you visited. Having the knowledge that you can send dishes back if you feel they were prepared improperly and that every kitchen has its own vision, you can say for sure in your review if they admitted it was a mistake or if it didn't personally fit your tastes. With this in mind, you can also avoid coming across as pretentious by not comparing it to another restaurant's dish of a similar name or ingredient.

Now, whether you're writing a positive or negative review, ask yourself whether you are writing to build up or tear down. Did you have a wonderful time but are marking the place down because its soap dispenser was automatic instead of manual? Did you have a lousy experience despite using the knowledge of this book? Think about the popularity of the "celebrities read mean tweets" and realize we do something similar on almost a daily basis. If you're being nasty just to be nasty, odds are your review is not going to be taken seriously, and you're probably going to be mocked by strangers. However, knowing how to differentiate and offer genuine constructive criticism will almost assuredly get to the right people and may improve your next experience there or the experiences of others, and in the end, isn't that what everyone wants?

SECTION 8

THE DIGESTIF

That's it! You made it through! Now that your brain is packed full of insider knowledge, it's time for you to try some real-life application! I would like to thank you, or whoever bought this book for you, for allowing me to shed some light on a subject that doesn't get the attention it deserves.

I wanted to keep this book as concise as possible so you could carry it in your back pocket while still relaying all the information anyone would need, and I feel I've succeeded in that respect. If you feel I've left something out or just want to send some general hate mail, feel free to contact me at author.jeremy.wilson@gmail.com.

Thanks for reading!